CHECKERBOARD BIOGRAPHY LIBRARY

EXPLORERS

Juan Ponce de
León

Kristin Petrie

ABDO
Publishing Company

visit us at
www.abdopublishing.com

Printed in the United States of America, North Mankato, Minnesota.
012007 042012

Cover Photos: Corbis
Interior Photos: Bridgeman Art Library p. 21; Corbis pp. 7, 14, 29; North Wind pp. 5, 9, 11, 12, 13,
    15, 17, 19, 20, 23, 27

Series Coordinator: Heidi M. Dahmes
Editors: Heidi M. Dahmes, Megan M. Gunderson
Art Direction & Cover Design: Neil Klinepier
Interior Design & Maps: Dave Bullen

Library of Congress Cataloging-in-Publication Data

Petrie, Kristin, 1970-
    Juan Ponce de León / Kristin Petrie.
        p. cm. -- (Explorers)
    Includes index.
    ISBN-10 1-59679-742-8
    ISBN-13 978-1-59679-742-0
    1. Ponce de León, Juan, 1460?-1521--Juvenile literature. 2. Explorers--America--Biography--
Juvenile literature. 3. Explorers--Spain--Biography--Juvenile literature. 4. America--Discovery
and exploration--Spanish--Juvenile literature. I. Title.

E125.P7P53 2006
972.9'02'092--dc22
[B]
                                                        2005048324

Contents

Eternal Youth

Have you ever heard of the Fountain of Youth? You may have heard your parents or grandparents joke about needing to visit this mythical place. Back in the 1500s, another person talked about finding the Fountain of Youth, too.

According to legend, Spanish explorer Juan Ponce de León crossed the Atlantic Ocean to find the Fountain of Youth. The fountain's water was said to heal the sick and give eternal youth. This may have been a perfectly good reason to cross the Atlantic. However, many historians believe Ponce de León sailed for different reasons.

Many Europeans dreamed of a better life in far-off places. Goods such as silk and gold came from these mysterious, distant lands. Surely, they thought, life was better where all of the beautiful things came from. They dreamed of wealth and power across the seas.

1271
Polo left for Asia

1295
Polo returned to Italy

1254
Marco Polo born

1275
Polo met Kublai Khan

Explorer Christopher Columbus introduced Europeans to the New World in 1492. Following his example, more explorers ventured into the unknown. When they returned home, they shared exciting stories. Ponce de León would also have stories from his big adventure.

Christopher Columbus discovered the route to the West. But, Juan Ponce de León discovered the Gulf Stream in 1513. This was the best way to return to Europe!

1460 or 1474
Juan Ponce de León born

1480
Ferdinand Magellan born

1324
Polo died

1475
Vasco Núñez de Balboa born

Noble Birth

Juan Ponce de León was born into an exciting time. The exact date of his birth is unknown. In fact, not even the year of his birth is certain. Some historians believe Juan was born in 1460, while others think the year was 1474.

Like his birthday, Juan's place of birth is also uncertain. But, it is believed he was born in Tierra de Campos Palencia. This village was in the León Province in northwestern Spain.

Not surprisingly, little is known of Juan's **heritage**. He is believed to have come from a noble family. This heritage gave him some advantages. Noble families sent their young sons to work for famous noblemen. This was part of a boy's education to become a knight.

1500
Balboa joined expedition to South America

1493
Ponce de León joined expedition to New World

1502
Ponce de León became governor of Higüey

**Juan was born in the province of León in northwestern Spain.
Today, this region is the country's leading producer of hops.**

1508
Ponce de León's first expedition

1514
Ponce de León knighted by King Ferdinand II

1513
Ponce de León's second expedition, discovered Florida and the Gulf Stream; Balboa was the first European to sight the Pacific Ocean

Young Juan

At a young age, Juan became a page to Pedro Núñez de Guzmán. At first, young Juan's duties were simple. He served meals and attended various events with Guzmán and his wife.

In exchange for his work, Juan learned to hunt, sing, and play the **lute**. He also received religious instruction. But most important, he learned to ride a horse. This skill would be vital in future battles.

When Juan entered his teenage years, he became a squire. As a squire, Juan's duties increased in importance. He cared for Guzmán's armor. Juan also learned how to use a sword and a lance. And, he accompanied Guzmán in battle. This was good preparation for a future soldier.

In 1492, Juan went to Granada, Spain. There, he fought the **Muslims**. The Muslims had ruled in Spain for nearly 700 years. But that year, Juan helped remove the last of this group from power.

1520
Magellan discovered the Strait of Magellan

1554
Walter Raleigh born

1519
Magellan led expedition to Spice Islands; Balboa died

1521
Ponce de León's third expedition, died in Cuba; Magellan died

After a long battle, the Spanish defeated the Muslims. On January 2, 1492, King Boabdil surrendered the kingdom of Granada to King Ferdinand and Queen Isabella.

Exploration

In the late 1400s, many courageous Europeans took to the water. Some explorers set out in search of more land for their countries. Others were just curious about what lay beyond the horizon.

The need for a new route to the Indies, or southeast Asia, was yet another reason for exploration. The Indies were home to the silk, gold, and spices that Europeans treasured.

Just one year after Juan helped remove the **Muslims** from power, Christopher Columbus returned to Spain. This explorer had big news. He claimed to have reached the Indies by sailing west across the Atlantic Ocean.

Back in Spain, Columbus became a hero. He was quickly granted a second voyage to the newly discovered land. Many believe that Juan's career as an explorer began in 1493. They think he jumped at the chance to join Columbus's second voyage to the New World.

1580
John Smith born

1585
Raleigh knighted by Queen Elizabeth I

1565
Henry Hudson born

1584–1589
Raleigh sponsored expeditions

Would you have signed up to travel with Columbus? Do you think Ponce de León was nervous about the trip?

Conquistador

Columbus's second expedition was an impressive undertaking. Ponce de León must have been excited when he reached the port at Cádiz, Spain. Seventeen ships had been prepared for the voyage. A crowd of 1,500 men waited to board them.

Men of all trades surrounded Ponce de León. Sailors and navigators would lead them across the sea. Many soldiers and knights went for adventure. Priests aimed to spread Christianity. They would all work to establish a colony in the New World.

Explorer Christopher Columbus claimed to have reached the Indies in the Pacific Ocean. He was wrong. Columbus actually found islands in the Caribbean Sea. These islands are now called the West Indies.

1595
Raleigh led first expedition

1588
Raleigh helped defeat the Spanish Armada

1606
Smith joined expedition to North America

When Ponce de León stepped on board, he became a **conquistador**. He probably aimed to become wealthy from the gold that was promised in the New World. And, maybe he would become powerful by conquering native peoples. In any case, he was ready for this adventure.

Cádiz is a major port city on Spain's southern coast.

Island Hopping

Ponce de León's first sea voyage began on September 25, 1493. That day, Columbus's second expedition set sail. For three weeks, the 17 ships crossed the vast Atlantic Ocean.

Ponce de León and his shipmates rejoiced when they sighted land. On November 3, the **fleet** reached an uncolonized island. Columbus claimed it for Spain and named it Dominica. Continuing on, Columbus led his fleet by many other new islands.

In mid-November, the ships approached another island. Columbus noted lush forests and beautiful beaches. He named the island San Juan Bautista. Today, we know this

In the late 1400s, Puerto Rico was home to 20,000 to 50,000 Taino.

tropical paradise as Puerto Rico. Columbus and the fleet did not stay long. They were eager to see what else was ahead of them.

1607
Hudson's first expedition

1609
Hudson's third expedition

1608
Hudson's second expedition

1610-1611
Hudson's last expedition, he died

Would You?

Would you have been able to cross the great Atlantic Ocean without getting seasick? How would you handle being on a ship for weeks on end?

By 1500, explorers sailed in caravels. These ships used square sails as well as traditional triangular sails. And, they allowed for longer sea voyages.

1614
Smith led expedition to North America, charted and named New England

1616
Raleigh's second expedition

Hispaniola

The **fleet** continued on and finally arrived at the large island of Hispaniola. In 1492, Columbus had left the first Spanish settlers there. These 39 men had stayed behind to guard La Navidad **stockade**.

When Columbus returned to La Navidad on his second voyage, he was shocked. The stockade was ruined. Ponce de León and the other passengers could not find any Spaniards alive.

Still, Columbus was on a mission. He established a new settlement to the east of La Navidad. He called the new settlement Isabela.

After this, little is known of Ponce de León's activities during the next few years. Some historians believe he remained on Hispaniola as a hardworking soldier. Others believe he returned to Spain for a time.

1618
Raleigh died

1637
Jacques Marquette born

1645
Louis Jolliet born

1631
Smith died

1643
René-Robert Cavelier de La Salle born

Many people believe that La Navidad's first settlers began fighting with each other after Columbus left. The Spaniards also treated the native Taino poorly. In time, the Taino fought back. They burned La Navidad.

Rough Times

If Ponce de León stayed in Isabela, he experienced rough times. The men were not used to the **subtropical** weather. Most of them wanted to get rich quickly and return to Spain. They were not interested in the amount of labor required for building a settlement and farming. The men grew frustrated.

To try to improve matters, Columbus sent men inland to search for gold to mine. Unfortunately, there was little gold to be found. Columbus was in trouble. He had to send gold to Spain to please King Ferdinand II.

In 1496, Columbus's brother founded Santo Domingo on Hispaniola. By this time, gold had been discovered near that area. So, Columbus forced the native Taino into hard labor. He had them **pan** for gold. And if they did not find enough gold, he punished them.

Not surprisingly, the natives grew tired of the harsh treatment. Soon, they began to fight back. It is known that Ponce de León helped fight the natives.

1669
La Salle explored Ohio region

1666
La Salle sailed to Canada

1673
Marquette and Jolliet explored the Mississippi River

Would You?

Would you have been brave enough to venture out into the unknown for a chance to find gold?

In 1492, the Spanish settlers had observed the Taino wearing gold jewelry. So, they knew that gold could be found on Hispaniola. When Columbus returned to Spain, he boasted about the wealth he had found.

Governor

In 1502, Ponce de León defended Spaniards against a native uprising. The Spaniards defeated the Taino. As a reward, Ponce de León was made governor of a new **province** called Higüey.

Ponce de León was given land and slaves to start his own plantation. His plantation flourished. And in 1505, he founded Salvaleon and built a large stone house. By this time, Ponce de León had married a Spanish woman named Leonor. They eventually had four children.

Ponce de León quickly became rich by selling supplies to ships headed to Spain. The cassava bread he sold was especially important. It stayed good the entire time it took to cross the Atlantic!

1675
Marquette died

1679
La Salle's first Mississippi River expedition

Ponce de León made a fortune on Hispaniola. But, it seemed to him that more profitable opportunities lay on a nearby island. He had heard reports of gold on Puerto Rico.

So, the explorer led a small expedition to Puerto Rico in 1508. King Ferdinand allowed Ponce de León to colonize the island. He founded the colony's oldest settlement, Caparra. This is near present-day San Juan.

King Ferdinand II

Then, Ponce de León returned to Hispaniola. He was named governor of Puerto Rico. But after a short time, he was replaced. He may not have minded this change, however. Ponce de León dreamed of even more adventure.

1682
La Salle's second Mississippi River expedition

1687
La Salle died

1684
La Salle's third Mississippi River expedition

1700
Jolliet died

Florida

In 1512, Ponce de León planned an expedition to search for an island called Bimini. Natives had told him he would find much wealth and the Fountain of Youth there. King Ferdinand granted Ponce de León permission to explore this legendary place.

Ponce de León assembled his **fleet**. He set sail from Puerto Rico with three ships in March 1513. The fleet sailed north, exploring the Bahamas along the way.

In April, Ponce de León reached the coast of what he thought was another island. He named it Florida. They first landed near present-day St. Augustine on the east side of the large **peninsula**. From there, Ponce de León directed his ships south. They explored the entire eastern coastline.

Ponce de León found himself fighting the currents of the **Gulf Stream**. He then explored the Florida Keys. After rounding Florida's southern tip, he explored and named the Dry Tortuga Islands. Then, Ponce de León led the expedition up the western coastline. He ended the search near Charlotte Harbor.

1770
William Clark born

1786
Sacagawea born

1774
Meriwether Lewis born

1800
Sacagawea captured

Would You?

Would you have believed that there was a fountain that could keep you young forever? If so, would you have gone out searching for it?

This is how Florida may have looked to Ponce de León and his crew. While sailing around Florida, they encountered the seven islands that make up the Dry Tortugas. "Florida" and "Tortugas" are the oldest European place names found on modern U.S. maps.

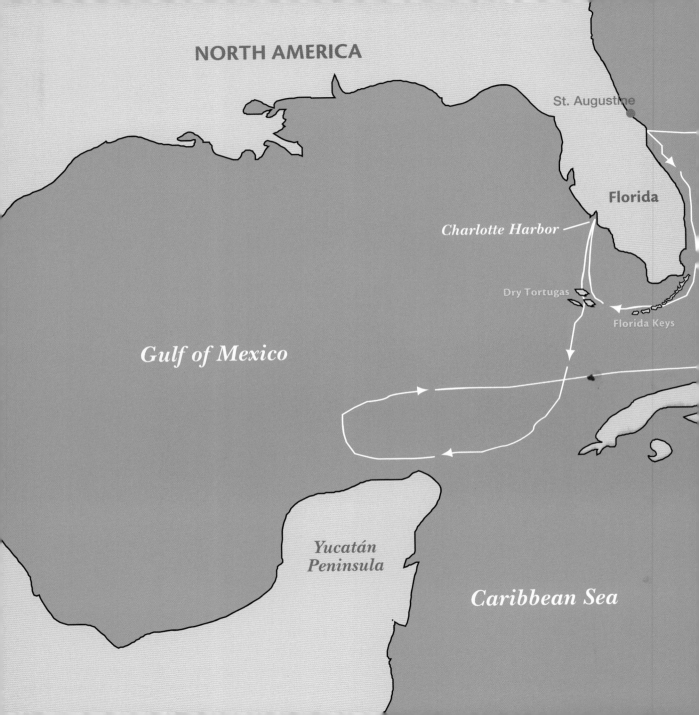

North Atlantic Ocean

The Journey of Ponce de León

1513 →

Bahamas

Cuba

Hispaniola

Puerto Rico

Jamaica

N

A Second Look

Ponce de León's expedition slowly made its way home. The **fleet** reached Puerto Rico in October 1513. It had been a successful trip. Ponce de León had discovered Florida and many of the islands that make up the Bahamas.

Ponce de León sailed to Spain in 1514 to report his findings. King Ferdinand was pleased. Ponce de León was knighted and given a personal **coat of arms**. King Ferdinand named him military governor of Florida. And, he allowed Ponce de León to colonize the area.

But first, Ponce de León was forced to resume his military duties. He returned to Puerto Rico in 1515. There, Ponce de León led battles against the Carib Indians.

In February 1521, Ponce de León finally set out for Florida. His expedition included two ships carrying about 200 men. The group settled near Charlotte Harbor.

1804
Lewis and Clark began exploring the Pacific Northwest

1806
Lewis and Clark returned to Missouri

1805
Sacagawea joined the Lewis and Clark expedition

In July 1521, Ponce de León was wounded by a Seminole arrow. He died believing that Florida was an island.

In July, natives attacked the Spaniards, and Ponce de León was wounded. He received treatment in Cuba, but he died from his injury.

1812
Sacagawea died

1856
Robert Edwin Peary born

1809
Lewis died

1838
Clark died

1881
Peary entered the U.S. Navy

Lasting Legacy

Ponce de León never found the Fountain of Youth or the island of Bimini. However, his many other discoveries more than made up for this.

Ponce de León does not get a lot of credit in Florida's history. This may be because he did not colonize Florida or explore inland. Nevertheless, he was the first European to record its sighting.

Another accomplishment to be noted was Ponce de León's discovery of the **Gulf Stream**. This strong current made sailing between the Americas and Europe faster!

Juan Ponce de León's legacy is most celebrated in Puerto Rico. On this island, he ruled fairly. And he founded strong cities, including Puerto Rico's capital, San Juan. Ponce de León is buried there at the San Juan Cathedral. From Puerto Rico to Florida, the Spanish **culture** introduced by Ponce de León and other courageous Spanish settlers lives on.

1893
Peary's first expedition

1909
Peary's third expedition, reached the North Pole

1905
Peary's second expedition

1920
Peary died

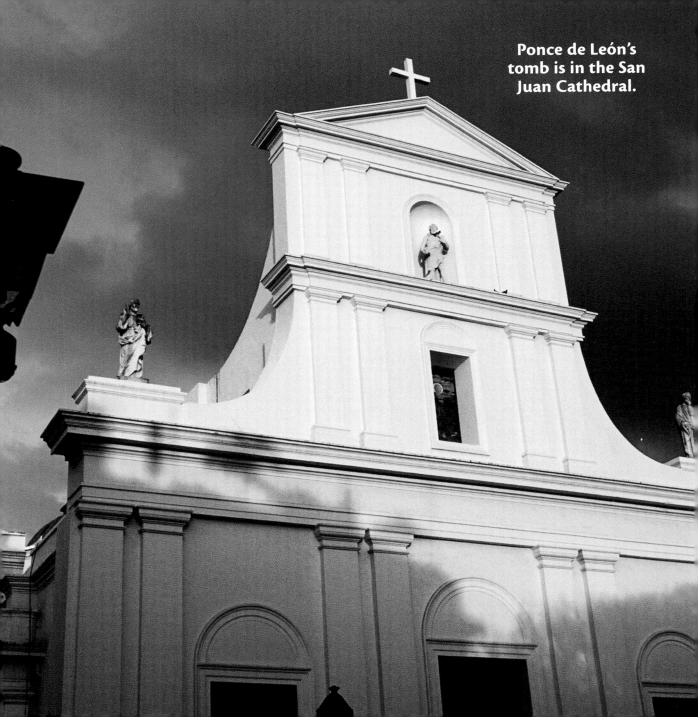

Ponce de León's tomb is in the San Juan Cathedral.

Glossary

coat of arms - a shield or other surface bearing symbols or words that represent a person's history and achievements.

conquistador - a leader in the Spanish conquest of the Americas.

culture - the customs, arts, and tools of a nation or people at a certain time.

fleet - a group of ships under one command.

Gulf Stream - a swift, warm current in the North Atlantic Ocean. It affects Europe's climate.

heritage - the handing down of something from one generation to the next.

lute - a stringed musical instrument with a pear-shaped body, ridges across the fingerboard, and a head that is angled back from the neck.

Muslim - a person who follows Islam. Islam is a religion based on the teachings of the prophet Muhammad as they appear in the Koran.

pan - to separate gold or other precious minerals from gravel by washing in a pan.

peninsula - land that sticks out into water and is connected to a larger landmass.

province - a geographical or governmental division of a country.

stockade - a defensive barrier made up of tall posts, usually forming an enclosure.

subtropical - a region bordering a tropical zone. A tropical zone is warm enough for plants to grow year-round.

Cádiz - KAH-theeth

conquistador - kahn-KEES-tuh-dawr

Higüey - ee-GWAY

Hispaniola - hihs-puhn-YOH-luh

Palencia - pah-LEHN-thyah

Taino - TEYE-noh

To learn more about Juan Ponce de León, visit ABDO Publishing Company on the World Wide Web at **www.abdopublishing.com**. Web sites about Ponce de León are featured on our Book Links page. These links are routinely monitored and updated to provide the most current information available.

Index